God Chose Me Study Guide

God Chose Me Study Guide

Untouchable Confidence for the Unstoppable Christian

Charles H. Metcalf III

WaterBrook

WaterBrook

An imprint of the Penguin Random House Christian Publishing Group,
a division of Penguin Random House LLC

1745 Broadway, New York, NY 10019

waterbrookmultnomah.com
penguinrandomhouse.com

A WaterBrook Trade Paperback Original

Portions of this work originally appeared in *God Chose Me*, copyright © 2025 by
Charles Henry Metcalf III, published in the United States by WaterBrook,
an imprint of Penguin Random House Christian Publishing Group,
a division of Penguin Random House LLC, in 2025.

Trade Paperback ISBN 978-0-593-60321-5
Ebook ISBN 978-0-593-60322-2

The Cataloging-in-Publication Data is on file with the Library of Congress.

Printed in the United States of America on acid-free paper

2 4 6 8 9 7 5 3 1

The authorized representative in the EU for product safety and compliance is
Penguin Random House Ireland, Morrison Chambers,
32 Nassau Street, Dublin D02 YH68, Ireland. https://eu-contact.penguin.ie

BOOK TEAM: Editor: Drew Dixon • Production editor: Helen Macdonald •
Managing editor: Julia Wallace • Production manager: Mark Maguire •
Copy editor: Lisa Grimenstein • Proofreaders: Bailey Utecht, Drew Goter

Book design by Virginia Norey

For details on special quantity discounts for bulk purchases,
contact specialmarketscms@penguinrandomhouse.com.

Contents

Contents

God Chose Me Study Guide

INTRODUCTION

Welcome to the study guide for my book *God Chose Me.* This study guide is designed to work in many different situations—including small groups, book discussion groups, or on your own as you walk through your healing journey. It is meant to serve as a companion to *God Chose Me,* where I share true stories and practical principles for those on the journey toward living a life with untouchable confidence. In this guide, we'll do a deep dive into the concepts laid out in my book, with an emphasis on gaining wisdom from God's Word.

I encourage you, as you work through this book, to be intentional not only in completing the exercises but also in allowing them to transform your thinking. If you treat this merely as a checklist of tasks accomplished, you will significantly diminish the opportunity to embrace a beautiful new life. So take a deep breath and be patient and present. Commit to walking through this study guide with honesty and intentionality, and see how God shows up.

How to Use This Guide

If you haven't already read *God Chose Me,* I encourage you to do so as you work through these sessions. The content is structured for a twelve-week study. Engage with the principles we'll explore, and reflect on how they relate to and apply to *your* life.

Remember to allow yourself—and God!—the time and space to work on your heart and mind. Even if you are meeting with a group, it will be beneficial to work through the sessions on your own first.

The Group Experience

God didn't design us to go through life alone, and that especially applies to life in the Spirit. The journey from insecurity to resting in God's love is best taken together, so, if possible, find a couple of friends to walk with you. We need fellow believers to help us live a Jesus-shaped life.

For a group setting, this guide will work best if you complete each session prior to meeting so that you can spend your time together in discussion. Each session includes enough material for about an hour of meeting time, though you can adapt the length to your group's needs. Whether you are the group leader or a participant, be kind, sensitive, and respectful of the other people in your group. Facing the damage left by rejection is hard! Courage comes and goes, and each person's journey has its ups and downs. Do all you can to create a place of safety and love so that everyone can receive what the Spirit is so ready to give.

Session Format

Each session includes three sections:

1. *Word:* Read, meditate, and reflect on a passage of Scripture. The Bible clearly states that God's Word is the only firm foundation upon which we can build our lives. As we begin to step into the confidence God calls us to, we must lean into and rely on the truth of His Word. Take time to read, re-read, and then read again if necessary to gain understanding. Seek help from a friend or one of my personal favorites, Google. Ultimately, allow God's Word to replace and renew the areas within you that need to embrace the confidence that only He can provide.

2. *Work:* Anywhere worth going requires work. And work is not bad; it's beautiful. Sit with each question and let it guide you in identifying the effects rejection and insecurity have had on your life. This might bring up some discomfort, or even pain, because rejection isn't God's intention for us; we're not built for it. But pay attention to the painful areas—they will show you where God wants to heal you. As much as you are able, share your thoughts and insights with those in your group.

3. *Wait:* The Bible tells us that those who wait on the Lord shall be renewed and find new strength (Isaiah 40:31). Throughout this study, take some time to

wait on God and allow yourself to find new strength. This is a perfect opportunity to journal and acknowledge new findings. Pray through the thoughts, feelings, and issues that come up throughout the study. Let the Holy Spirit guide you and heal you. Lasting restoration involves God's Spirit helping us understand who He made us to be (and who we already are, even if we don't believe it yet!): loved, chosen, and empowered for purpose.

A Note for Leaders

If you're leading a small group through this guide, I encourage you to do some extra preparation to ensure your group time is as profitable as possible. As you work through each session on your own, take notes and mark the questions that are not only most meaningful to you but also those that might be important for your group to discuss.

Consider consulting a study Bible for any pressing questions that arise as you work through the Scriptures. However, do not feel like you need to have the answers to every question your group members might ask. The goal of meeting together is to grow in relationship with God and with one another, not to have all the answers. Don't be afraid to say, "I don't know, let me get back to you" if a question comes up in your group time that you don't know how to handle.

Most importantly, pray. Before you meet with your group to discuss each session, spend some time praying for your group members by name if possible. Ask God to meet each member as they work through the material. Ask Him to heal wounds, instill confidence and contentment, and move you all to greater love and faithfulness.

BE PRESENT AND PATIENT

In the prologue of *God Chose Me,* it says, "Whatever you are hoping to get or change about yourself from reading this book is not nearly as important as being present in and to this moment" (page 8). Exactly who and where you are now is exactly when and where God wants to work—not in the past (though He can heal that) and not in the future (though He has a plan for that), but right here in the present.

So practice bringing your wandering mind and heart to be present right here, right now—because here and now is where God is present to *you.* Practice trusting the future to the God who loves you and chose you (which means you can afford to be patient rather than worrying that you're not further along on your journey). You're right where you need to be.

Take a deep breath. And another. And maybe one more just to be sure.

Okay. The study guide starts now.

You Are Loved at Your Lowest + This Is What God Does

Based on chapters 1 and 2 of God Chose Me

I n chapter 1, "You Are Loved at Your Lowest" (page 18), I wrote:

> You are loved—where you are, who you are, how you are. If you never beat the addiction, if you never do "the right thing," if you stay in this exact spot, you will still be loved. This love is unexplainable. It defies reason. That is because it is not an earthly love but one that finds its source in *the* source of all light and love. It is not yours to earn. It can only be accepted.

Does that feel true to you right now, in this moment? If so, go ahead with the next section. If not, take a few minutes to be patient and present with your doubts. In your journal or in the space below, make a quick list of all the reasons God's love for you doesn't feel real or possible. You don't need to change or solve anything right now; just let yourself become aware of your doubts.

_____

_____

_____

_____

Later, in chapter 2 (pages 25–26), I wrote:

> Do you feel foolish, weak, or lowly? Friend, I've got good
> news. You are the ideal candidate to be chosen and used
> by God to turn the world upside down. . . .
> You are perfectly positioned to see the power of God
> move in your life.

The good news of these first couple of chapters is this: Your
doubts about God's love don't change a thing. You're right
where you need to be.

WORD

Read Psalm 103, out loud if possible. Explore a few Bible translations to get a fuller picture of what this passage reveals about
God and about you.

After you've finished reading, sit quietly for a minute or two.
In our loud, hurried, hyperconnected world, being still is a radical act that helps us make space for God. Just be here, right
where you are. Don't even check your phone. Once you've
spent some time reflecting on this passage, jot down a few
things Psalm 103 says about your relationship with God.

_____

_____

As you meditate on this psalm, what emotions arise for you? Assurance? Disbelief? Hope? Fear? Write them all down, even if they're confusing or conflicting. Note which lines in the psalm provoke a particular feeling in you. (For example, verses 15 and 16 might inspire calm or fear, depending on the person.) Take five to ten minutes with this exercise. The goal is to determine where you are when it comes to your trust in God's unfailing love and loving intentions toward you.

_____

_____

_____

_____

_____

_____

WORK

1. In chapter 1 (page 12), I shared about a season in my life when I felt panicky, fearful, and far from God:

I could no longer see His hand or feel His love. I grew cold, empty, and hopeless, becoming a shell of the joy and laughter I once carried. . . . It was as though I had a slow leak in my tire. I found myself stranded in a place I did not recognize, with no clear way out.

Maybe you haven't felt exactly like that, but everybody has emotional lows in their life. When was the last time you experienced a season of deep insecurity, anxiety, loneliness, doubt, or shame? (It's okay if it's right now!) What were the factors, both around and within you, that contributed to that difficult or painful season?

_____

_____

_____

_____

_____

_____

2. "When I felt the least worthy, the least capable, the least qualified, and least likely to be chosen, it was at that very moment I realized I am still loved" (page 15). This realization sounds similar to Psalm 103:4, where God "redeems your life from the pit and crowns you with love and compassion." Why do you think it might be more important to experience and accept God's love when you're at your lowest rather than when you're winning?

_____

_____

_____

_____

_____

_____

3. I hope right now you can be open and honest in this safe space because "the things we think disqualify us from being chosen are the very things God is planning to use in our lives" (page 27). What are those things for you—the actions, attitudes, hurts, or sources of shame that tempt you to believe you're worthless, useless, or unlovable?

_____

_____

_____

_____

_____

_____

4. "What you've been through has the potential to be the most powerful part of your testimony. Once you recognize that you are chosen and believe that you are known, accepted, and loved, you have nothing to lose and everything to gain" (page 29). Using your holy imagination—which is a gift from God and one of the Holy Spirit's favorite places to inspire and guide you—allow yourself to envision how God might use the actions, attitudes, hurts, or sources of shame you listed in question 3 to reveal His goodness and glory.

_____

_____

_____

_____

_____

God chose you. Your past does not define you. Your shortcomings are not the limiting factor, and your mistakes are not too big for God to use. Inversely, your successes do not define you either. Your greatest days are not behind you! If you will dare to surrender your plan and path to God, He has something far better for you. He stands ready to bring beauty out of every broken part of your life. . . . When you are chosen, your past does not disqualify you; in fact, it is the very thing that equips you for His purpose.

—*God Chose Me* (pages 30–31)

WAIT

Take a few deep breaths.

To cope with everyday life, many of us ignore our feelings of insecurity and inferiority—which means it can be hard, scary, and exhausting work to intentionally address those negative emotions and experiences. Although it might be difficult to believe right now, it's worth it! God shines the light of healing on anything we're willing to expose to His loving gaze. But even more than that, He promises to be with us every uncomfortable step along the way. Remember what Psalm 103 says: The Lord's love is with you "from everlasting to everlasting" (verse 17).

As you spend some time in prayer, open your heart and mind to sense His presence with you. Right here, right now.

LET'S PRAY

Use the following prayer as a starting point for expressing yourself to our loving God. (The journaling space on the following page is also available for recording your thoughts.) Whatever you're feeling, whatever your doubts and confusion, let Him know. He's safe. There's nothing you can say that will shock our creator.

God, I believe that You are with me.
Or at least, I want to believe it.
Give me courage to attend to the hurts and mistakes of my past
and trust that You have a plan and purpose to redeem each one.

Teach me to be humble instead of hiding
and bring trustworthy companions to journey with me.
I want to know You and Your love for me.
Help me believe and trust.

In Jesus's name, amen.

NOTES

THE UNSTOPPABLE MOVEMENT + HE KNOWS YOU . . . AND HE STILL CHOSE YOU + THE REJECT EFFECT

Based on chapters 3, 4, and 5 of God Chose Me

Chapter 3 is all about how untouchable confidence requires deep commitment to the unstoppable movement of Jesus: "A confidence that cannot be moved only comes with the kingdom that cannot be shaken" (page 43). In this session, I want to connect the commitment Jesus expects of us to His perfect knowledge of us. Toward the beginning of chapter 4, I wrote, "God, the creator of the universe, knows who you are. The Scriptures go so far as to say He knows the number of hairs on our heads" (page 49). Does this feel like good news or bad news to you right now? Why is that?

_____

_____

_____

_____

And consider this from chapter 5 (pages 62–63):

> The reason rejection cuts us at such a deep level is that it was never a part of the plan. It goes against the core truth of the human soul. Somewhere deep down, we know we deserve to be accepted. We know we should be loved and cared for—and not for what we do but simply for who we are. . . . We were created to be seen, valued, and loved.

If bringing past rejections to the forefront of your mind makes you feel anxious as we tackle these chapters, keep grounding yourself in this bedrock truth: God knows you and chose you anyway. In other words, no matter who you are, where you are, or what you've done in the past, Jesus invites you to sell out to His unstoppable movement. And when you do, you'll find a level of confidence you never thought possible!

WORD

Read Psalm 27, out loud if possible. Use several Bible translations to get a better idea of what this passage says about trusting fully in God's care and provision.

After you've finished reading, sit quietly for a minute or two. Set your phone aside and be still and quiet as you make space for God. Just be right here, right now.

As you meditate on Psalm 27, can you relate to the psalmist's joyful confidence? Or does it seem too good to be true? (Or is it somewhere in between?) Choose two or three verses that capture how you'd like to feel, and rewrite them in your own words, including details from your life and situation. For example, you may not have armies besieging you or enemies oppressing you, but it's likely you've felt under attack.

_____

_____

_____

_____

_____

_____

_____

WORK

1. The focus of chapter 3 is the unshakable confidence that comes from knowing that our king, Jesus, is unstoppable. Think back to the many examples of people in the Bible and throughout history who had an unshakable confidence because of their faith in Jesus. Which examples stand out most to you? Why?

_____

_____

_____

_____

2. In chapter 4, I wrote, "To be fully loved, you must first be fully known. In fact, I would say that it is almost impossible to love someone completely until you know them fully—the best and the worst parts" (page 51). Many of us believe deep down that if people knew the "real" us, we would be rejected. What parts have you kept hidden for fear of rejection?

_____

_____

_____

_____

_____

3. "God has chosen you not despite knowing you but *because* He knows you. He knows you better than you know yourself. He knows that who you think you are is far from the fullest picture of who you *truly* are. He knows you so well He believes not in your worst habits but in your greatest potential. God knows you and He still chose you" (pages 51–52). So, who do you think you are? Take a moment and write down what you really think of yourself. When you're done, prayerfully ask God to show you why that's not the whole story. What does God believe about you that is truer than what you believe?

_____

_____

_____

_____

4. In chapter 5, I wrote, "What did you love that seemed to make it hard for others to love you? . . . We all have our 'green moment,' the moment we realized we didn't fit. . . . It's the moment you began to believe that something in you is broken" (page 57). Most of us have experienced rejection more than once, but is there one rejection that stands out to you as your "green moment"? What happened? How did you react?

_____

_____

_____

_____

5. "What have you changed about yourself, what lies have you told, what stories have you believed, what beauty have you suppressed in hopes of avoiding that feeling of being rejected?" (page 60). Our instinct is to do just about anything to avoid rejection—even change ourselves. What have you changed or masked to feel accepted?

_____

_____

_____

_____

You do not have to live in the aftermath of your rejection. You do not have to remain a victim of others' words. You do not have to continue to shy away from who you are supposed to be. You do not have to lessen yourself just to stay in that relationship. Today you can make one of the greatest decisions of your life. . . . You can step into a life where you are not defined by the words of others but by the grace and word of God over your life. . . . *You may have experienced rejection, but you are not rejected.* You are completely and wholly accepted by God.

—*God Chose Me* (page 64)

WAIT

Take a few deep breaths.

Facing the painful parts of our past does not feel good. Yet it is good and necessary work—and we don't have to do it alone. As I said in chapter 5, *"The seed of rejection in the soil of insecurity always produces the fruit of the fake you. . . .* If you do not allow God to replace the soil of your heart, you will never be able to grow" (pages 59 and 62). God's Spirit is willing and waiting to perform healing in you, at your invitation.

If you're ready, spend some time in prayer.

LET'S PRAY

Use the written prayer below as a starting point for your own expression. (You can also use the journaling space on the following page to record your own prayer.) After you've spent some time talking to God, try listening. What, if anything, do you hear God's Spirit whispering to your spirit? If you're not sure, consider asking a godly, trustworthy friend to pray with you, and then share your thoughts.

God, it's painful to deal with the past.
Part of me wants to keep ignoring what You want to heal.
But I hear Your call in my heart to surrender,
and I want to trust You.

I want to trust that You know me and You chose me.
"Though my father and mother forsake me,
the LORD will receive me" (Psalm 27:10).
Teach me to be that confident in You, Lord.

In Jesus's name, amen.

NOTES

A Singular Symphony

Based on chapter 6 of God Chose Me

"Many times my soul has felt like an out-of-tune and out-of-time orchestra that cannot find the same note. It feels like every instrument is fighting for a solo or simply lacking direction" (page 67). Like me, you might resonate with this feeling of internal discord. We often try to silence certain instruments in our life's orchestra—maybe the melancholy violin of our struggles or the crashing cymbals of our enthusiasm that we fear might be too much for others.

But remember, "the best symphonies find their power in juxtaposition—the beauty of multiple parts coming together to express one sound" (page 67). The same is true of you and me. We are not meant to be simple melodies but instead complex symphonies conducted by the Master Musician Himself. Every part of you—even the parts you try to silence or tune out—has a place in God's orchestra.

_____

_____

_____

_____

WORD

Read 1 Corinthians 12:12–27, out loud if possible. Explore a few different Bible translations to get a fuller picture of what this passage reveals about unity in diversity. While Paul's focus was on unity in diversity in the church, there is also a lesson here about the very heart of God. And when you realize how God values unity and diversity, you may also see that there is a lesson in this passage for you personally. As you consider how Paul used the metaphor of a body, with each part essential and worthy of honor, examine how this might apply to the different aspects of who you are.

After you've finished reading, sit quietly for a minute or two. Resist the temptation to check your phone. Just be present to this moment with God's Word. Think about how God, as three persons in perfect unity, created you to reflect His own beautiful complexity.

As you meditate on this passage, notice how Paul emphasized three key truths:

1. Every part belongs (no part can say "I don't belong").

2. Every part is necessary (no part can say "I'm not needed").

3. Every part deserves honor (even the parts we think are weaker).

Take five to ten minutes to reflect on how these truths apply to you. Which parts have you been saying "don't belong"? Which parts have you been trying to silence or hide?

_____

_____

_____

_____

_____

_____

WORK

1. In chapter 6, I shared about the photos on my book's back cover—snapshots of different aspects of who I am. The broken man under the desk, the Kentucky cowboy, the father, the husband, the dreamer in the Iverson jersey. If you were to take photos representing different aspects of yourself, what would they be? Write a brief description of each "snapshot," including the parts you readily show others as well as the parts you tend to hide.

_____

_____

_____

_____

_____

_____

2. "We are complex individuals with many different facets and talents. We carry the complexity and beauty of God in our very makeup" (page 68). Think about how the Trinity models unity in diversity. God the Father (Creator), God the Son (Savior), and God the Spirit (Helper) work in perfect harmony while maintaining distinct roles. What different roles and aspects of yourself need to find similar harmony? How might seeing yourself as created in the image of the triune God change how you view your complexity?

_____

_____

_____

_____

_____

_____

3. In this chapter, I presented this question: "Will anyone accept all of me? If I stopped switching and pretending and was just me—all of me—what would happen?" (page 72).

What keeps you from showing all of yourself? What would it look like to trust that God not only accepts but chooses *all* of you—every instrument in your personal symphony?

_____

_____

_____

_____

_____

4. Look at the "Be Both" section from the chapter. Which pairs resonate with you? What parts of yourself have you been treating as *either/or* that could become *both/and*? Create your own list of "be both" statements that apply to your life.

_____

_____

_____

_____

_____

You are a divine symphony. You are many beautiful parts that all deserve to be expressed in the right tune and tone. Perhaps life has convinced you that there aren't many

people who would fully love you if they fully
knew you—but God is the one person who
can accept all of you.
            —*God Chose Me* (page 76)

WAIT

Take a few deep breaths.

Imagine yourself as that orchestra I described earlier—every instrument, every note, every rhythm representing a different aspect of who you are. Now picture God as the conductor, bringing all your parts into harmony. He doesn't silence any instrument; He doesn't remove any section. Instead, He knows exactly when each part should shine and how they all work together.

"As you surrender to God as the conductor of your life, this surrender not only changes you but also releases those around you" (page 77). When we let God conduct our lives, when we stop trying to silence certain instruments or force others to play too loudly, we create space for those around us to do the same.

I mentioned that my friend Mike is "so himself that he gives others the power to be themselves" (page 77). That's what happens when we let God conduct our symphony: We become so secure in who we are—every part included—that others feel free to be fully themselves too.

Stay present to His presence with you—right here, right now, as you continue this journey of aligning your words with His truth.

LET'S PRAY

Using the prayer below to get started, thank God for each part of you (even the parts you may not like or accept). This isn't an exercise in self-acceptance; it's an acknowledgment of your creator. Give thanks for all your diverse parts, and begin to trust that God knows just how to make them harmonize.

Father God, Master Conductor,
thank You for creating me with such complexity,
for making me more than just one note,
for choosing every part of who I am.

Help me surrender every instrument to You:
the loud cymbals of my enthusiasm,
the quiet strings of my vulnerability,
the steady percussion of my strength.

Make my life a symphony that draws others
into the freedom of being fully themselves.
Let every note I play declare Your glory
as it invites others into Your acceptance.

In Jesus's name, amen.

NOTES

You'd Be Surprised What a Little Belief Can Do + Better Watch Your Words

Based on chapters 7 and 8 of God Chose Me

In chapter 7, I wrote about watching *Space Jam* as a kid, believing I could fly. But that childlike belief didn't apply to just basketball—it reflected something deeper that lies in all of us. As I shared, "Belief . . . has the power to take humans to places that no one thought possible. It fuels dreams and provides hope for a reality we cannot yet see" (page 82).

But belief isn't just about positive thinking. It needs to be watered with confession—speaking God's truth over our lives. That's why my wife and I created daily confessions for our children. Because "when your confession changes, so do your beliefs—and when your belief changes, so do your actions" (page 94). In this session, I want to guide you through developing your own confessions to water and strengthen your belief that God chose you.

_____

_____

WORD

Read Hebrews 11:1–6, out loud if possible. Use several Bible translations to get a more complete picture of what this passage reveals about the connection between faith, belief, and pleasing God. Notice especially how each person mentioned acted on their belief through concrete steps of faith.

As you meditate on this passage, consider how each person's faith was expressed through both belief and action. What did they have to declare as truth before they could step out in faith? Take ten minutes to write down what you need to believe—and declare—about God and yourself so that you will have faith to step toward God's calling.

_____

_____

_____

_____

_____

WORK

1. "Your belief either *cripples* your reality or *cultivates* it" (page 84). Think about the beliefs you currently confess over your life, whether consciously or unconsciously.

What messages do you repeat to yourself? Which ones
need to change? Write down your current beliefs and the
truths you need to start declaring instead.

_____

_____

_____

_____

_____

2. Let's develop your personal confessions. The goal here is
to acknowledge and declare who God says you are and
who God made you to be. Remember: "These statements
are written with the understanding that you cannot do
anything by yourself. That without Christ you do not
have the strength, peace, and purpose that you need"
(page 103). Write one confession that aligns with each of
the following categories:

- Your identity in Christ
- Your purpose and calling
- Your relationships and connections
- Your growth and development
- Your faith and trust in God

_____

_____

_____

_____

_____

_____

3. I shared some of our family confessions: *"Metcalfs carry . . . Peace and Purpose, Kindness and Compassion . . ."* (page 93). What do you want your family to carry? What qualities, values, and truths do you want to be known for? Write these down as declarations, not just wishes.

_____

_____

_____

_____

_____

4. "The secret to sustaining a belief is consistent confession" (page 94). What practical system or routine can you put in place to keep these confessions active in your life? When and where will you speak them? How will you remember them? Consider writing them down, setting phone reminders, or creating visual prompts in your space.

_____

_____

_____

_____

_____

_____

Your words create worlds. But do you like the
world you have created?
                    —*God Chose Me* (page 98)

WAIT

Take a few deep breaths.

As I said in the book, "The very power that spoke the Milky
Way into existence . . . resides in you" (page 103). You're not
just making empty declarations—you're partnering with God's
creative power to speak His truth over your life. These confessions you've just written aren't wishful thinking; they're seeds
of faith planted in the soil of God's promises.

Think about my son, Arlo, declaring "Boldness and Bravery"
(page 94) before trying something new. Nothing about his situation changed, but his confession gave him strength to move
forward. In the same way, speaking your confessions in God's
presence isn't about changing your circumstances instantly. Instead, it's about aligning your heart with His truth and letting
that truth change how you see yourself and your situation.

Take a moment to speak one of your confessions softly. Notice how it feels in your heart and mind. If it feels uncomfort-

able or untrue, that's okay—remember what I wrote about my own journey: "I still must choose to believe that I am chosen" (page 89). Growth starts with small steps of faith, with declaring truth even before we fully believe it.

Stay present to His presence with you as you align your words with His truth.

LET'S PRAY

Take time now to pray through your newly written confessions. Speak each one slowly, letting it sink into your spirit. Remember, "Your confession does not have to be accurate to have authority" (page 94). You're not describing what is; you're declaring what will be through God's power.

Father God, thank You for the power of belief,
for the authority You've given my words,
and for the privilege of declaring Your truth
over my life and family.

Help me write confessions that align with Your Word,
declarations that echo Your promises,
statements that strengthen my faith
and water the seeds of belief.

Give me courage to speak life,
even when circumstances say otherwise.
Help me remember that my mic is always on,
that You hear every word I say.

Let these confessions become more than words,
more than positive thinking or empty hopes.
Let them be anchored in Your truth
and empowered by Your Spirit.

In Jesus's name, amen.

NOTES

READY WHEN YOU ARE

Based on chapter 9 of God Chose Me

Remember the story I shared about my wife saying, "Ready when you are!" after taking forever to get dressed? My (overly) dramatic response revealed something deeper about readiness, especially when it comes to God. As I wrote, "Many of us have believed what I think could be one of the most misleading misconceptions, and that is: 'You are waiting on God'" (page 112). The truth is, more often than not, God is waiting on us.

Think about it: We spend so much time asking God for things we're not prepared to receive or manage. We ask for bigger opportunities while neglecting the small ones in front of us. We pray for expanded influence while avoiding the responsibility we already have. Instead, "We must shift our perspective so that every day of our lives we wake up and live with a spirit that sees each day as an opportunity to prepare" (page 114).

_____

_____

WORD

Read 1 Samuel 3:1–10, out loud if possible. Explore a few different Bible translations to get a fuller picture of what this passage says about being ready to hear and respond to God's voice. Notice how Samuel needed help learning to recognize God's voice and how his readiness developed into one of the simplest but most powerful prayers: "Speak, LORD, for your servant is listening" (verse 9).

After you've finished reading, sit quietly for a minute or two. Engage in the radical act of refusing to be distracted. Be present to this moment.

As you meditate on this passage, consider Samuel's journey to readiness:

- He was in position (serving in the temple)
- He was attentive (hearing the call multiple times)
- He was teachable (learning from Eli)
- He was willing (responding with openness)

Take ten minutes to reflect on your own readiness. Where are you positioned? How attentive are you? Are you teachable? Are you willing?

_____

_____

_____

_____

_____

_____

_____

WORK

1. "If God said to you, 'Ready when you are,' what would be your response?" (page 112). Be honest—what's your first reaction to this question? What areas of your life feel ready for God to move? What areas need more preparation?

_____

_____

_____

_____

_____

_____

_____

2. Think about the personal confessions you developed earlier. (If you haven't created these yet, refer to session 4 as a guide.) How might these declarations need to shift or expand to reflect a spirit of readiness? For example, if one of

your confessions is "I am chosen," could it become "I am chosen and ready for whatever God asks"?

_____

_____

_____

_____

_____

_____

3. Remember what I wrote about Noah: "At some point Noah had to make the decision to believe God, but then his decision had to turn into preparation" (page 115). What specific preparations could you begin today for the dreams God has placed in your heart? Think practical steps, not just spiritual hopes.

_____

_____

_____

_____

_____

_____

4. "What if God took your preparation for marriage, for college, for kids, for growth, for finances, for love, for ministry and used that as the measuring bar for what to give you? Would you like what you receive?" (page 117). Choose one area of your life to examine closely. What would intentional preparation look like there?

_____

_____

_____

_____

_____

_____

What if you began each day with a purpose in your spirit and joy in your heart, saying, "Today could be the day everything changes. Today could be the day God comes through." . . . When you decide to live with this expectation, it shifts your life from passivity to preparation. You start seeing and living in the reality you are hoping for rather than where you feel stuck.

—*God Chose Me* (page 115)

WAIT

Take a few deep breaths.

Keep in mind what I wrote about God's timeline: "God's timeline and our timeline are roughly 27 quintillion miles apart" (page 113). Yet He still invites us to prepare, to be ready, to position ourselves for what He wants to do. Being ready isn't about perfect timing—it's about a prepared heart.

Stay present to His presence with you. Let His nearness prepare you so that you are ready.

LET'S PRAY

Take a moment to review your personal confessions. Pray them slowly, letting each one sink in. If you haven't developed these yet, that's okay—use this time to ask God what declarations He wants you to begin making over your life and/or the lives of your family members. Consider how each confession might shift to reflect not just who you are but also your readiness for what God wants to do through you. Use this prayer as a starting point for your own conversation with God.

Father God, like Samuel I want to say,
"Speak, for your servant is listening" (1 Samuel 3:10).
Make me ready—not just willing
but prepared for whatever You ask.

Help me see each day as training, each moment as preparation,
each small step of obedience as practice for bigger assignments.

Shift me from passive waiting to active preparation.
From asking for things I'm not ready for
to becoming ready for things I haven't asked for.

Let my confessions be more than words;
let them shape my readiness.
Let my declarations lead to action
and my faith lead to preparation.

When You say, "Who will go?"
let me be positioned to say, "Here I am!"
When You say, "Ready?"
let me truly be able to say, "Ready!"

In Jesus's name, amen.

NOTES

I'm Not Afraid to Live

Based on chapter 10 of God Chose Me

"I ain't afraid to live and I sure ain't afraid to die!" (page 121). I yelled those words during a prayer service at my church, and I meant them—at least I thought I did. Less than twelve hours later, God gave me the opportunity to prove it when a car crashed into me during my morning bike ride. As I wrote, "It happened so fast and yet somehow also seemed to happen in slow motion" (page 120). Sometimes our boldest declarations get tested in ways we never expect.

That accident shook my confidence and forced me to wrestle with a crucial question: *"Will fear steal my future?"* (page 121). It's easy to live unafraid when everything feels safe. But what about when life (occasionally in the form of a motor vehicle) reminds us that nothing is truly risk-free? What about when God calls us to something that feels uncertain?

The truth is, as I discovered through my accident and recovery, there's a profound difference between living safe and living secure. Living safe means avoiding risk at all costs, calculating every move, and staying within comfortable boundaries. But living secure in God means something entirely different. "You can choose to live safe and reserved or secure and ridiculous" (page 124). When we know we're chosen by God, we can take risks not because we're guaranteed safety but because we're guaranteed the security of His presence.

_____

_____

_____

_____

_____

WORD

Read Philippians 1:18–26, out loud if possible. Read a few different Bible translations as you try to "hear" the apostle Paul's joy and urgency in this passage. When you're done reading, sit for a few moments in radical, rebellious silence that pushes against a culture trying to distract you from what's truly important.

Imagine yourself in Paul's place: imprisoned, facing execution, unsure of what each new day will bring. As you meditate on Philippians 1, consider what you would write to a group of fellow Christians if you were in such dire circumstances. How would your letter be different? How would it be similar?

_____

_____

_____

_____

_____

_____

_____

WORK

1. In chapter 10, I wrote, "Life is full of risk, and risk means there is a chance of failure. As we examine our lives, we must face the reality that life is full of what I call 'NSAs,' or 'Non-Safe Activities'" (pages 122–23). What are some of the NSAs you're trying to avoid in your life?

_____

_____

_____

_____

_____

_____

2. "Many people today have created this politically correct, whitewashed Jesus who asks us to do only normal, safe, easy things. But Jesus called His followers to 'take up their cross and follow [Him]' (Matthew 16:24). Jesus's message and Jesus's people have always been marked by a level of ridiculousness" (page 125). Think back to the Jesus you were first introduced to, whether it happened years ago or just recently. What words would you use to describe Him? How does the Jesus of the Bible compare with the Jesus you learned about?

_____

_____

_____

_____

_____

_____

3. "This is the track record of God. He is constantly calling us *out* of safety, *out* of our security. Out of the shadows and the boxes we create to protect ourselves. . . . Our savior is not safe, nor is the life He calls us to live" (page 125). Why do you think God calls His children (us) away from safety and comfort? What do you think He might be trying to accomplish in and through us?

_____

_____

_____

_____

_____

_____

4. In this chapter, I challenged you to "ask yourself these two questions: *What if?* and *Why not?*" (page 129). What would you be doing differently if these were your go-to questions (instead of *What if it goes wrong?* and *Why would God choose me?*)? Take a few minutes and come up with ways to keep these questions in mind. Consider adding them to your phone reminders, writing them on sticky notes, or sharing them with a trusted friend.

_____

_____

_____

_____

_____

_____

You were not created to pursue a life of safety and security. You were created to do the impossible. To break molds and patterns. To turn the world upside down with a confidence and fire that is not concerned with what looks acceptable. You were not meant to live shy, scared, and safe. You were meant to have a spirit that looks for the impossible and expects God to show up. When you truly

believe that you have been chosen by God,
there is a security that envelops your soul
and begins to ignite a trust in Him that does
not look for the safest route.

—*God Chose Me* (pages 125–26)

WAIT

Take a few deep breaths.

Fear is inevitable; it's part of our God-installed protection system. So feeling shame about it is a waste of time and energy! Instead, shift your focus to God, trusting that He is bigger than your fears. If He's guiding you to do something risky (an NSA, for example), maybe it's because your comfort or dignity isn't His only or primary objective. He's got bigger dreams for you! As you spend time in His presence now, offer your fears to Him. Rest in the assurance that you, your fears, your dreams—all of you—are secure in His love and care.

Let's Pray

Use the following prayer as a starting point for expressing your fears and hopes to the God who loves you.

Jesus, I know You are not a "safe" savior.
But You are trustworthy
and faithful.

My fears and anxieties tell me to play it safe,
but You tell me to trust in You.
Give me courage, Lord.
Make me brave enough to "do it scared."

I want to fulfill the potential You put in me
before I was born, the destiny You have planned
just for me.
Please don't let my fears stand in the way.

Thank You for being faithful even when I'm fearful.

In Jesus's name, amen.

NOTES

HE CHOSE . . . ME?

Based on chapter 11 of God Chose Me

In chapter 11 (page 131), I addressed embracing both confidence and humility:

> The statement "God Chose Me" should encourage and develop a posture of humility, not pride. Gratitude, never an attitude. Reverence, not arrogance.

Have you ever felt the tension between confidence and humility? Take a moment to reflect on whether you tend to lean more toward pride or self-deprecation when thinking about being chosen by God. There's no wrong answer—just be honest with yourself about where you are right now.

_____

_____

_____

_____

WORD

Read John 15:1–17, out loud if possible. Explore several different Bible translations to get a better understanding of what this passage reveals about being chosen by Jesus.

After you've finished reading, sit quietly for a minute or two and make space for God. Don't allow yourself to be distracted! Just be with Him, right here.

As you meditate on this passage, pay special attention to verse 16: "You did not choose me, but I chose you and appointed you so that you might go and bear fruit." What emotions arise when you read those words? Joy? Disbelief? Unworthiness? Write them down, noting which phrases trigger particular feelings. Take some time with this exercise. The goal is to honestly assess how you feel about being chosen by Jesus.

_____

_____

_____

_____

_____

_____

WORK

1. In chapter 11, I shared how I felt like being chosen by God was "too good to be true" (page 137). The fact that God

would want me and use me seemed impossible given my weaknesses and failures. When have you found it hardest to believe that God really chose you? What situations or thoughts make you question your "chosen" status?

_____

_____

_____

_____

_____

_____

2. "Our awareness of our weakness can either lead to a retreat from God or a reverence for God" (page 134). Think about a current weakness or struggle in your life. How might God want to use that very thing to draw you closer to Him? What would it look like to let your weakness produce reverence instead of retreat?

_____

_____

_____

_____

_____

_____

3. "When you focus on yourself, the only result is a spiral of insecurity and shame that pulls you away from God. . . . However, when you turn your focus from the power of your weakness to the power of your God, a unique shift happens" (page 136). Describe a time when you got stuck focusing on yourself and your failures. Now imagine reframing that situation through the lens of God's power and God choosing you. How does the story change?

_____

_____

_____

_____

_____

4. "I am called by God, and He could've chosen anybody. I am insanely gifted, and I am equally as frail" (page 137). This is the power of "yes, and" that I talk about in this chapter. Write some "and" statements that describe the beautiful tension in your own life as someone chosen by God. (For example: "I struggle with anxiety, *and* I carry God's peace" or "I've made huge mistakes, *and* I am completely forgiven.")

_____

_____

_____

_____

_____

_____

Friend, I pray you experience the deep gratitude of a moment like this daily. That you would pause long enough to look around at the blessings in your life and be honest with yourself. Honest enough to admit you couldn't have planned this. Honest enough to realize that no matter how organized you are, you aren't organized enough. To realize that every good thing in your life is a miracle. May you recognize how God has taken your mess and made a masterpiece, and may you say, "God Chose Me."

—*God Chose Me* (page 138)

WAIT

Take a few deep breaths.

There's profound mystery in being chosen by God—that He knows everything about us and still wants us. It can feel too good to be true, causing us to either puff up with pride or shrink back in shame. But God invites us to a different way: humble confidence. As you spend time in prayer, sit in that tension. Let yourself be amazed by His choice of you while remembering that it's all grace, all a gift.

Stay present to His presence with you. Right here, right now.

Let's Pray

Let this time of prayer be focused on praise and thanksgiving. It's hard to be arrogant when you're full of gratitude! Use the following prayer to inspire your own expressions of praise.

Jesus, I am in awe that You chose me,
not because I earned it or deserved it
but simply because You wanted me.

Help me walk in the tension
of confidence and humility,
neither shrinking back nor puffing up
but resting in the miracle of being Yours.

When I start to doubt or question Your choice,
draw my attention back to Your faithfulness.
Let every weakness become a reminder
of Your strength and Your grace.

Thank You for choosing me.
Help me live worthy of that choice today.

In Jesus's name, amen.

NOTES

GET UP, DONNIE!

Based on chapter 12 of God Chose Me

I opened this chapter by talking about how confusing the Bible can be—particularly the book of Job. Even though I've read Scripture since I was five and have taught it for more than a decade, I still have more questions than answers. And you know what? That's okay. In fact, it's in wrestling with these difficult stories that we often discover the deepest truths about God and ourselves.

Remember what I shared about Job's story: "God does one of the most confusing and frustrating things I have ever seen in Scripture. He volunteers Job to the devil! He brings him up as though He is bragging to the devil, saying, 'He's the best one I got!'" (pages 140–41). This may challenge our thinking about what it means to be chosen by God. Sometimes being chosen means being chosen for difficulty—but that difficulty always has purpose.

When it comes to resilience and your source of strength, "the revelation 'God Chose Me' is the strongest why for your resilience" (page 147). That's because when God is your why, you tap into something far deeper than willpower or determination. You connect to the very power that raised Christ from the dead.

Take a moment to reflect: When life knocks you down, what typically motivates you to get back up? Is it willpower? Pride? Fear? Or have you found a deeper source of resilience in knowing you're chosen by God? What would it look like to let God be your *why* in those moments?

_____

_____

_____

_____

WORD

Read Romans 8:31–39, out loud if possible. Read a few different Bible translations to get a more complete picture of what this passage reveals about God's unfailing commitment to those He has chosen. Pay special attention to the list of things Paul said cannot separate us from God's love: trouble, hardship, persecution, famine, nakedness, danger, and sword. These aren't just theoretical challenges; they're real-life knockdowns that believers face. And they're things you are likely to face in some manner in your life. However, none of these—not a single one—will separate you from the greatest gift in the universe: God's love.

After you've finished reading, sit quietly for a minute or two. Remember, being still helps us make space for God. Be here, right now. Let the weight of these words sink in: "If God is for us, who can be against us?" (verse 31).

As you meditate on this passage, focus especially on verse 37: "In all these things we are more than conquerors through him who loved us." What does it mean to be "more than conquerors"? This isn't about just surviving or barely making it through. It's about thriving in the face of adversity because we know who chose us. How does being chosen by God give you strength to get back up after being knocked down? What would it look like to approach your current challenges as more than a conqueror rather than just a survivor? Take five to ten minutes to journal your thoughts.

WORK

1. In chapter 12, I wrote about Job's story and asked, "If I were Job, at some point I would have asked myself, *Why am I chosen? Why is this happening to me?*" (page 143). When have you found yourself asking these *why* questions? What situation in your life right now makes you wonder, *Why me?* Be specific: What circumstances have you questioning God's choice of you? What losses or setbacks are making you doubt? Remember, it's okay to be honest about these questions. Even Job, whom the Bible calls blameless, wrestled with them.

_____

_____

_____

_____

_____

_____

_____

2. "Instead of asking *why,* I want you to ask *what.* We cannot control the why.... We have control over what" (page 145). Think about your current challenges. How might shifting from "Why is this happening?" to "What will I do now?" change your perspective and response? What specific actions could you take to move forward, even if you don't understand why you're in this situation? Start by asking, "What now?"

_____

_____

_____

_____

_____

_____

_____

_____

3. I shared three reasons we can get back up: "You owe it to you"; "you owe it to them"; and "you owe it to Him" (pages 148 and 149). Let's break these down:

1. You owe it to you because "you've come too far to come only this far" (page 148). What progress have you already made that you don't want to abandon?

2. You owe it to them because "whether you realize it or not, there are people watching your life" (page 149). Who might find hope in seeing you stand up again?

3. You owe it to Him because "you can stand up because Christ got up" (page 149). How does Jesus's resurrection give you hope and strength?

Which of these three resonates most strongly with you right now? Why? What would it look like to stand up again for that reason?

_____

_____

_____

_____

_____

_____

_____

_____

4. "Just like Donnie, you have a decision to make: Will you embrace your name? Will you embrace whose name is on you?" (page 152). The name you carry isn't just your family name or your given name—it's the name of Christ. What does it mean to you that you carry His name? How might embracing that identity give you strength to get back up? Think about how this might change your approach to:

- Your daily challenges
- Your relationships
- Your work or studies
- Your dreams and goals
- Your response to failure

_____

_____

_____

_____

_____

_____

_____

_____

The reason you can have resilience is not because you're perfect. It's not because life is easy. It's not because things are always going to go your way. You can be resilient because of the resurrection of Jesus. The Bible says that the same power that raised Christ from the dead lives inside of you (see Romans 8:11).
—*God Chose Me* (page 150)

WAIT

Take a few deep breaths.

Getting knocked down is part of life, but staying down is optional when you know who chose you. "I'm not sure what challenges you're facing. I'm not sure how many times you've been knocked down. But what I do know is there's a power within you that is stronger than the pain you're experiencing" (page 152).

As you spend time in prayer, let God's Spirit remind you of His resurrection power living in you. You don't have to manufacture the strength to get up—you just need to tap into the power He's already placed within you. This isn't about trying harder or being stronger. It's about surrendering to the One who chose you and letting His strength become yours.

Stay present to His presence with you. Right here, right now.

Let's Pray

Use this prayer as a starting point for allowing God to strengthen you.

Father God, thank You for Your resurrection power
living and active within me.
When I'm tempted to stay down,
remind me whose name I carry.

Give me strength not just to survive
but to stand up again and again—not because I'm so strong
but because You chose me.

Help me remember that my resilience
gives others hope to stand too.
Let my life show Your
power to get up after every fall.

When I'm questioning why,
help me focus instead on "What now?"
Guide my next steps forward,
even when I can't see the whole path.

Thank You that You never leave me down,
that Your strength never runs out,
that Your choice of me never wavers,
even when I struggle to stand.

In Jesus's name, amen.

NOTES

_____

_____

_____

_____

_____

_____

_____

_____

_____

_____

_____

_____

_____

_____

_____

_____

ALL I NEED IS A MEMORY

Based on chapter 13 of God Chose Me

One memory can change your future. This is especially true when it comes to remembering what God has done. The character Andy Bernard from *The Office* said, "I wish there was a way to know you're in 'the good old days,' before you've actually left them." In our journey with God, we're actually living in the "good old days" right now—we just need to recognize and remember His faithfulness along the way.

I explained in this chapter that "a memory triggers your focus. Your focus triggers a feeling. Feeling produces fruit" (page 155). Let's break that down:

- Memory: Recalling specific moments of God's faithfulness
- Focus: Where your mind and heart go because of that memory
- Feeling: The emotions that memory stirs up (gratitude, peace, hope)

- Fruit: The actions and attitudes that grow from that feeling

Think about that chain reaction for a moment. What memories of God's faithfulness immediately come to mind? What feelings do those memories stir up? Where does your focus go when you remember those times?

_____

_____

_____

_____

_____

WORD

Read Psalm 77, out loud if possible. Explore a few different Bible translations to get a more complete picture of what this passage reveals about the importance of remembering God's faithfulness. Notice how the psalmist moves from distress to hope by intentionally recalling what God has done. This psalm is particularly powerful because it shows us that remembering isn't just about feeling nostalgic; it's also about finding strength for today.

After you've finished reading, sit quietly for a minute or two. Be here now, with your memories of God's goodness.

As you meditate on Psalm 77, notice these key movements in the text:

- Verses 1–3: The psalmist's initial distress
- Verses 4–9: Wrestling with doubts and questions
- Verses 10–12: The turning point of choosing to remember
- Verses 13–20: Recounting God's mighty deeds

This is often how remembering works in our own lives. We start in a place of struggle, but as we intentionally recall God's faithfulness, something shifts. Remember: "When we pause to remember what God has done, we are intentionally taking a moment to stop and look back on the goodness of God" (page 158). Take a few minutes to write your own psalm following this pattern, recounting specific ways God has shown up in your life.

WORK

1. In chapter 13, I wrote about how "lying dormant within your memories could be the fruit, the future, and the fuel

you have been desperately searching for in order to live the life God called you to live" (page 156). Think about three specific categories of memories:

1. A time when God provided unexpectedly

2. A time when He gave you strength you didn't think you had

3. A time when He made a way when there seemed to be no way

For each memory, answer these questions:

- What was happening?
- How did God show up?
- What does this tell you about God's character?
- How might this memory fuel your faith today?

_____

_____

_____

_____

_____

_____

2. "During the many distractions of our lives, we often fail to realize the faithfulness and history we have with God.

When we feel stuck in our current situation, it can be easy to forget how God has consistently made a way time and time again" (pages 158–59). Let's apply the feeling-focus-fruit framework to your current situation:

- What situation is making you feel stuck right now?
- What memory of God's past faithfulness could help?
- What feelings does that memory stir up?
- How might those feelings help you focus?
- How might this produce fruit in your heart and life?

_____

_____

_____

_____

_____

_____

3. Just like God told the Israelites to set up memorial stones, we need physical reminders of God's faithfulness. "As they did this physical act, they were forced to remember what God had done for them. This was meant to spark gratitude, joy, and hope not only in their hearts but in the hearts of the children who would come after them" (page 159). Consider how you might create your own modern-day memorial stones. Start with something personal—perhaps a gratitude journal where you record answered prayers, or a special playlist of songs that mark significant moments with God. Think about physical spaces too. Maybe there's a place where you regularly meet with God or a corner of your home that could become a visual reminder of His faithfulness.

Remember, memorials aren't just for us as individuals. The Israelites built their memorial together, and we can do the same. Think about ways to weave remembrance into your family life or community. This might look like sharing stories of God's faithfulness during family meals, creating annual celebrations of significant spiritual moments, or writing letters to future generations about how you've seen God work. The key is creating tangible reminders that help both you and others remember God's goodness.

_____

_____

_____

_____

_____

_____

4. This chapter ends with a powerful declaration: "If He did it then, He can do it again" (page 159). This isn't just positive thinking—it's faith built on memory. Remember: "He is a way-making, chain-breaking, mind-restoring, heart-

healing, body-transforming, marriage-mending, purpose-giving, all-powerful God" (page 160). Take some time to reflect on how you've seen each of these aspects of God's character in your own life. When has He made a way where there seemed to be no way? What chains has He broken in your life? How has He renewed your mind or healed your heart? Think about times He's given you physical strength, mended your relationships, or revealed His purpose for your life.

Now consider where you need Him to do it again. What situations in your life right now need His way-making power? What still needs breaking, healing, or transforming? Write these things down, pairing each current need with a memory of His past faithfulness in that area. Let these memories fuel your faith for His future work in your life.

_____

_____

_____

_____

_____

_____

_____

_____

You may have worked hard to forget your past, and I am by no means asking you to dig up old wounds. However, I do believe that if you were to review the history of your life, you would recognize God's track record of faithfulness. As we reflect on our lives, we will start to remember and our souls will begin to feel hope and light, knowing that God always comes through.

—*God Chose Me* (page 159)

WAIT

Take a few deep breaths.

Memory isn't just about the past—it's fuel for the future. "There is an untapped resource of hope, joy, expectation, and faith that lies dormant in the recesses of your memory" (page 159). As you spend time in prayer, let God bring to mind the times He's shown up for you. Think about those moments when His presence was undeniable, when His provision was exactly what you needed, when His timing was perfect even though you couldn't see it at first.

Don't rush this process. Just as the Israelites had to physically pick up stones from the Jordan River, take time to carefully gather your memories of God's faithfulness. Let each one build your faith for what He wants to do next.

As always in these moments, stay present to His presence with you. Right here, right now.

LET'S PRAY

Father God, as I pause to remember,
I'm overwhelmed by Your faithfulness.
Every memory of Your goodness
becomes a stone of remembrance.

Thank You for the times You've made a way,
for the battles You've already won,
for the prayers You've answered,
for the strength You've provided.

When fear rises, help me remember.
When doubt creeps in, help me recall.
Help me treasure these testimonies of Your never-failing love.

Let my memories of yesterday fuel my faith for tomorrow.
Let Your past faithfulness light the path ahead.

May my life become a living memorial,
a testament to Your goodness,
a witness to Your power,
a story of Your choosing love.

For every miracle You've done before,
I trust You to do it again.
For You are the same God
yesterday, today, and forever.

In Jesus's name, amen.

NOTES

MY FRIENDS SAVED MY LIFE

Based on chapter 14 of God Chose Me

I started this chapter with my grandmother's wisdom: "If you hang with nine broke friends, you are bound to be the tenth one" (page 161). Of course, this isn't just about money—it's about the profound influence our friends have on our lives. I expanded on my grandmother's premise: "If you hang with nine people who have a bad attitude, you're bound to be the tenth. If you hang with nine friends who don't have integrity, you're bound to lower your standards" (page 168). But the beautiful thing is that this works in reverse too—when we surround ourselves with people who are pursuing God, we find ourselves drawn closer to Him as well.

I discovered this truth through years of moving schools and making new friends. At first, I kept people at arm's length because I knew we'd move again soon. "It was my own defense mechanism. This was my way of avoiding getting hurt" (page 162). But God has taught me something beautiful: "I have not had a ton of friends, but I have always had the right friends" (page 165). He brought the right people at exactly the right time—people who would shape my faith, encourage my growth, and sometimes even save my life.

Think about your own friendship journey. Have you found yourself keeping people at a distance? Or have you experienced the gift of having exactly the right friend at exactly the right time?

_____

_____

_____

_____

_____

WORD

Read Ecclesiastes 4:9–12, out loud if possible. Read from a few different Bible translations to get a fuller picture of what this passage reveals about God's design for friendship and community.

After you've finished reading, sit quietly for a minute or two. Remember, being still and quiet makes space for God. Just be here, right now.

As you meditate on these verses, notice the progression:

- Two are better than one (verse 9)
- One helps the other up (verse 10)
- Two keep warm together (verse 11)
- A cord of three strands is not quickly broken (verse 12)

Take five to ten minutes to reflect on how you've experienced each of these aspects of friendship. When has someone helped you up? When have you helped someone else? How have you experienced the strength of community?

_____

_____

_____

_____

_____

_____

WORK

1. In chapter 14, I wrote about how "the message of God choosing me is not one of isolation but relationships. This book is titled *God Chose Me,* but it could also be *God Chose Us*" (page 165). Think about a time when you tried to go it alone, "just me and Jesus." What happened? Now think about a time when you let others walk alongside you. How was that different?

_____

_____

_____

_____

_____

_____

2. Remember what I wrote about Jesus choosing friends: "If anybody had an excuse to not have friends—if anybody technically didn't need anybody—it would have been Jesus. But He chose to live in community" (page 166). What excuses do you make for keeping people at a distance? What might change if you followed Jesus's example of allowing yourself to need others?

_____

_____

_____

_____

_____

_____

3. Think about your current friendships. I shared that "God has graciously supplied me with friends who have supported me, encouraged me, and helped me follow Jesus" (page 165). Look at your friendships through these lenses: Who encourages your faith? Who challenges you to grow? Who do you trust with your real struggles? Who brings out the best in you? If you can't think of anyone in one of these categories, take time to pray about what kind of friends you need in this season.

_____

_____

_____

_____

_____

_____

4. "To Find a Friend, Be a Friend" (page 172) is one of the sections in this chapter. Proverbs 18:24 says, "A man who has friends must himself be friendly" (NKJV). What kind of friend are you right now? Think about what I shared regarding Pastor Mike, who "would always ignore what seemed like the most important thing, just to check on me" (page 169). When was the last time you checked on someone's heart rather than just their circumstances? What would it look like to be the kind of friend who shows up not just for the big moments but in the ordinary Tuesday mornings? Consider one person you could reach out to this week—not to get anything but just to be a friend.

_____

_____

_____

_____

_____

The greatest friends I've had are not those I simply shared interests with or who looked like me, voted like me, or talked like me. The greatest friends I've had were people who God placed in my life for a reason.
—*God Chose Me* (page 171)

WAIT

Take a few deep breaths.

Recall this from chapter 14: "Friends are different from family. You can't choose your family. . . . But friends are different—friends, you choose. God not only chose you, but He also chose you for the people you're around" (page 168). As you spend time in prayer, thank God for choosing you and for the people He's chosen to put in your life.

Let's Pray

Jesus calls us friends (John 15:15). Let that sink in. The God of the universe wants to be your friend. Stay present with that as you pray.

Father God, thank You for designing us for friendship,
for making us need one another,
for showing us through Jesus
what true friendship looks like.

Thank You for the friends who've shaped my life,
for those who showed up when I needed them,
for those who spoke truth in love,
for those who helped me follow You.

Help me be the kind of friend
who draws others closer to You.
Give me courage to be vulnerable
and wisdom to speak truth in love.

Open my eyes to see the people
You've already placed around me.
Give me strength to reach out,
to build deeper connections.

Thank You that You call me friend.
Help me live worthy of that title,
both with You and with others,
as we walk this journey together.

In Jesus's name, amen.

NOTES

IT'S NEVER TOO LATE TO COME HOME

Based on chapter 15 of God Chose Me

I saved this chapter for last when writing the book because, as I said, "for some reason, it feels the most important. This chapter holds a lot of weight in my heart" (page 173). You see, this isn't just another chapter about God—this is a love letter to anyone who's wandered far from home. Maybe you picked up this book by accident, or someone gave it to you and you're wondering how you ended up reading something with "God" in the title. Maybe just seeing that word stirs up anger, disappointment, or emptiness inside you. Maybe you used to believe but don't anymore or you're hanging on to faith by your fingernails.

I wrote this chapter for you. "This is not a book for just Christians. As a matter of fact, my personality is usually bent toward trying to offend Christians just a little bit (in love) because that's what I feel Jesus would have done" (page 174). I pray these words find their way to the outsiders, the misfits, the ones who feel too far gone or too broken to come home.

It's okay if you resonate with this: "You may read these words and still want nothing to do with God" (page 180). Really, it's okay. Just for this session, let's try to talk not as author and reader but as friends. Because whether you believe it or not, there's a Father waiting for you to come home.

_____

_____

_____

_____

_____

Word

Read Luke 15:1–2 and Luke 15:11–32, out loud if possible. Explore a few different Bible translations to get a fuller picture of what this famous story reveals about God's heart for those who have wandered far from home.

After you've finished reading, sit quietly for a minute or two. Be still, refusing to let distractions steal your attention.

As you meditate on this story, put yourself in different characters' shoes. Have you felt like the younger son, wanting to get as far from home as possible? Like the father, watching and waiting for someone beloved to return? Or perhaps like the older brother, resentful of grace given to others? Take five to ten minutes to write down what strikes you most about this story and why. Who do you identify with most?

_____

_____

_____

_____

_____

_____

WORK

1. I wrote that "we have wandered so far for so long, some of us can't even recognize the path that would lead us home" (page 176). How do you feel far from home right now? It might be in your relationship with God, with others, or even with yourself. What makes the journey back feel impossible?

_____

_____

_____

_____

_____

_____

2. Think about the prodigal son's journey. "He prepared an apology, a long list of the ways he'd wronged his father, and slowly began to drag his feet back toward home" (page 177). What apologies or explanations do you feel like you need to make before you can come home to God?

Now consider the father's response: no explanations needed, just pure love and celebration. How does this challenge your view of returning to God?

_____

_____

_____

_____

_____

_____

3. For some, "the reason you avoid God is because you have lied to yourself about the quality of life you're living" (page 181). Be honest with yourself: Are you truly content with life away from God? What emptiness are you trying to fill with other things? I wrote that "when you slow down long enough to feel the pain inside of you, you realize your soul is fractured to a point that money, sex, drugs, and influence cannot fix" (page 181). What would it cost you to admit you miss home? What keeps you from acknowledging that deeper hunger in your soul?

_____

_____

_____

_____

_____

_____

4. "Sometimes it's hard to receive grace. Sometimes we feel unworthy or like we need to earn it. *That is not the gospel*" (page 182). Where in your life are you trying to earn what God wants to freely give? Remember what I wrote about settling for being a servant: "The truth is, there are a lot of people who follow Jesus who have settled for servant. . . . Their whole walk with Him is built on this false humility and shame that keeps them stuck with their head down and no hope" (pages 181–82). What would it look like to simply receive His grace like the prodigal son received his father's embrace? To let yourself be not just forgiven but fully restored as a son or daughter?

_____

_____

_____

_____

_____

_____

_____

_____

God is kind, God is gracious, God is loving, God is accepting. God is holy. God cares about you and the pain you're experiencing. And no matter what people have told you, no matter who has abandoned you, and no matter how they have misrepresented His love, do not allow the mistakes of people to rob you of living in your true home.

—*God Chose Me* (page 180)

WAIT

Take a few deep breaths.

Reflect on what I wrote about the father in Jesus's story: "Every single day the boy's father had sat waiting for this day—the day his son came home" (page 178). Your Father in heaven is waiting just like that, scanning the horizon for any sign of your return. "He knew it was his son. He'd observed that boy's shoulders since he was a toddler. He knew how the boy hung his head when he'd been hurt" (page 178). That's how well your Father knows you too.

You don't have to clean yourself up first. You don't have to have the right words. You don't even have to be sure about everything. "You'll be surprised at what happens when you arrive. You won't be met with shame or guilt. You'll be met with a hug, grace, and mercy" (page 181). You just have to take one step toward home.

LET'S PRAY

Father God, thank You for waiting,
for watching the horizon,
for running to meet me
even when I'm still far off.

Thank You that You don't demand
perfect words or complete understanding.
You don't require me to earn
what You freely give.

Help me see past the lies
that keep me far from home.
Past the hurt others have caused,
past my own fear and shame.

Give me courage to return,
even if all I can do is crawl.
Give me faith to believe
that You'll still receive me.

Thank You that home is not a place
but a person—You.
And You are never far,
always ready to welcome me back.

In Jesus's name, amen.

NOTES

UNTOUCHABLE

Based on chapter 16 of God Chose Me

Congratulations! You've made it to the final session. "You may have put this book down and picked it back up several times, or you may have just powered your way through—but either way, you were strong, consistent, and you finally made it to the very end" (page 184). But reaching the end isn't really the end, is it? It's actually the beginning of something new—the place where truth meets transformation.

I confessed something important in this chapter: "As much as I believe this book can change you, I can't *promise* this book will change you" (page 185). Why? Because knowledge alone isn't enough. We live in a culture that's drowning in information but starving for transformation. What we need isn't more facts but "revelation that turns into action . . . action that turns into a lifestyle" (page 187). We need truth that changes not just what we know but how we live.

That's where we find ourselves now—at the intersection of learning and living. Will "God Chose Me" be just another interesting concept you once read about, or will it become the foundation you build your life upon?

_____

_____

_____

_____

WORD

Read Joshua 1:1–11, out loud if possible. Explore several Bible translations to get a fuller picture of what this passage reveals about God's call to courageous living. Notice especially how God frames His command to Joshua to "be strong and courageous": It comes with both a mission (enter the land) and a promise (the Lord will be with you).

After you've finished reading, sit quietly for a minute or two. Consider how Joshua might have felt in this moment. Moses was dead, the Jordan River stood before them, and hostile nations awaited them in the Promised Land. Yet God's command wasn't "Be safe" but rather, "Be strong and courageous." If you were in Joshua's shoes, how would you feel?

_____

_____

_____

_____

As you meditate on this passage, notice the three times God told Joshua to be strong and courageous (verses 6, 7, and 9). Each time comes with a different emphasis:

- In taking possession of the land (verse 6)
- In obeying God's law (verse 7)
- Because God is with you (verse 9)

Take a few minutes to reflect on areas of your life where you need this same courage. Where is God calling you to step out? Where do you need to obey even when it's hard? Where do you need to remember He's with you?

_____

_____

_____

_____

_____

WORK

1. "You can now begin to enter the space every human soul deeply desires: the unique grace at the intersection of confidence and contentment" (page 188). That's where we've been headed all along, remember? As you look back over the book's chapters and the eleven previous sessions, identify one or two ideas, realizations, or practices that

stand out as most significant for your life. Allow those to be where God begins your transformation. Where can you start turning information into wisdom?

_____

_____

_____

_____

_____

2. When it comes to confidence ("a sense of sureness, readiness, humility, inner strength. Not born from self but received from God," [page 188]), where did you start with this study and where are you headed? As you've journeyed with me through *God Chose Me*, have you seen a change in your confidence? Try to put into words what is changing.

_____

_____

_____

_____

_____

3. What about contentment ("a settled soul. A rested mind. A heart that needs nothing more than to simply be with God," [page 188])? How you felt yourself changing when it comes to experiencing "a deep sense of gratitude and appreciation for the moment you're in and where you are" (page 188)?

_____

_____

_____

_____

_____

_____

4. The subtitle of my book is *Untouchable Confidence for the Unstoppable Christian*. Take a moment and consider what might be holding you back from living with more confidence. How might knowing that God loves you and chose you help you overcome this roadblock?

_____

_____

_____

_____

_____

_____

I pray this message is wind in your sails. I pray this belief is fire in your bones. I pray that your sense of self finds its anchor deep below the shallow counterfeits this world has to offer. I pray comparison feels as useless as a sweater in August. That your mind is as free as a bird in springtime. I pray your heart beats strongly as one that is full of purpose. That your eyes see beyond tomorrow and into the legacy you leave behind.

—*God Chose Me* (page 190)

WAIT

Take a few deep breaths.

As we conclude in prayer together, let's keep ourselves open to the ways God wants to continue working in us. If we allow it, this end can be a new beginning.

LET'S PRAY

God of goodness and love,
thank You for choosing me.
It's still hard to believe sometimes,
but it feels a little truer now than before.

I choose You too.
Even when doubts arise
and circumstances spin out of my control,
give me courage to choose You.

Give me the confidence that comes from being loved
and the contentment that comes from a habit of trust.
As You transform me, give others hope that
they can be transformed too.

Draw me closer to You,
because that's where You've chosen for me to be.

In Jesus's name, amen.

NOTES

© MAXWELL SHAVERS

About the Author

CHARLES METCALF is the executive pastor of Transformation Church in Tulsa, Oklahoma, where he serves alongside Pastor Michael Todd. Charles and his wife, Abby Rose, have four beautiful children, Arlo Phoenix, Luna Rose, Jade October, and Blue Sunday. Instagram: @charlesmetcalf.

About the Type

This book was set in Albertina, a typeface created by Dutch calligrapher and designer Chris Brand (1921–98). Brand's original drawings, based on calligraphic principles, were modified considerably to conform to the technological limitations of typesetting in the early 1960s. The development of digital technology later allowed Frank E. Blokland (b. 1959) of the Dutch Type Library to restore the typeface to its creator's original intentions.

From author and pastor
CHARLES METCALF

Learn to harness the power of your words, build meaningful relationships, and recover from life's setbacks. This transformative book offers a road map to living authentically and confidently, empowering you to fulfill your unique, holy purpose.

This companion study and discussion guide to *God Chose Me* will propel you toward your God-given purpose with joy and clarity. Discover how embracing your chosen status can revolutionize your self-perception and daily life.

WATERBROOK

Learn more about Charles Metcalf's books at
waterbrookmultnomah.com.